Text by Frederick C. Klein

For the Love of the
Red Sox

An A-to-Z Primer for Red Sox Fans of All Ages

Illustrations by Mark Anderson

"In my first few years with the Red Sox, people used to compare me to **Phil Rizzuto** and **Pee Wee Reese**. It wasn't quite on the same level as the arguments about whether **Ted Williams** was better than Joe DiMaggio, or who was the best center fielder, Mickey Mantle, Willie Mays, or Duke Snyder, but there were debates, especially in Boston and New York, over which of us was the best shortstop. Rizzuto and Reese are both in the Hall of Fame, and they both deserve to be there. I'm in the Boston Red Sox Hall of Fame, and that's good enough for me, especially now that they are world champions.

And speaking of the Red Sox Hall of Fame, most of the other players in this unique book are there too. I hope you enjoy reading about them, some of the greatest Red Sox players of all time, accompanied by the wonderful illustrations, which bring the players and their eras to light."

—Johnny Pesky

"A" is for "At last!" —

The Sox fans' collective cry
When the Cardinals were beaten
And the trophy held high.

THE BOSTON RED SOX ENDED 86 YEARS OF FRUSTRATION in spectacular fashion during the 2004 season, coming back from a three-games-to-none deficit to defeat their archrivals, the New York Yankees, in the American League Championship Series and then sweeping the St. Louis Cardinals in four games in the World Series. The Yankees series stood out because no previous major league baseball team had won a best-of-seven postseason set after losing the first three games. The previous Red Sox World Series triumph had come in 1918. Between then and 2004 the team had been to the championship round three times without success.

"B" is for Babe Ruth.

The team sold him, and worse,
Had to live 86 years
With the Bambino's curse.

GEORGE HERMAN "BABE" RUTH came to the major leagues in 1914 at age 19 as a left-handed pitcher, and in that capacity helped the Red Sox win the World Series in 1915, 1916, and 1918. Short of cash, the team sold him to the New York Yankees for $125,000 in 1920. In New York, where he was moved to the outfield full time because of his batting ability, "the Bambino" rewrote baseball's power-hitting records and led the Yanks to numerous championships. His so-called curse was a sports-page invention, but 1918 remained the Red Sox's last World Series title until 2004.

"C" is for Clemens,

Whose nickname is "Rocket."
This fastballing Texan
Had fans in his pocket.

ROGER CLEMENS joined the Red Sox in 1984 out of the University of Texas, and went on to tie the great Cy Young for the team's all-time pitching record with 192 wins over the next 13 seasons. Big and hard-throwing, the right-hander won the American League best-pitcher awards named for Young in 1986, 1987, and 1991, and led the league in strikeouts three times. His later career with the New York Yankees earned him two World Series rings.

"D" is for Damon,

Who, Samson-like, gained strength
From his hair and his beard,
Which were just the right length.

JOHNNY DAMON caused a stir by sporting an unballplayer-like full beard and mustache for much of the 2004 season, but he more than fulfilled expectations on the field. The veteran center fielder and leadoff man led the team in hits (189) and stolen bases (19) during the regular season. In the ALCS versus the Yankees he scored the winning run in the team's come-from-behind fifth-game victory, and drove in six runs on two homers, including a grand slam, in the clinching seventh game. In the World Series against the Cardinals, his first-inning home run sparked the 3–0, fourth-game victory that brought the title to Boston.

DOMINIC DIMAGGIO and
BOBBY DOERR were career-
long Red Sox who were teammates
on the 1946 American League
champion team.

"E" is for Evans,

A right fielder with class.
No gardener ever
Covered more grass.

DWIGHT EVANS played for the Red Sox from 1972 through 1990. He ranks second in club history for most games played (2,505) and is among the team's top 10 in just about every career hitting category. He was an eight-time Gold Glove winner at his demanding position. He had great fielding range and base runners rarely challenged his arm.

"F" is for Fisk,

Who kept Sox hopes alive
With his barely fair homer
In '75.

CARLTON "PUDGE" FISK, born in Bellows Falls, Vermont, started at catcher for the Red Sox from 1972 through 1980, winning All-Star Game berths in seven of those seasons. He is best known for his home run off the left-field foul pole at Fenway Park in the twelfth inning of Game 6 of the 1975 World Series, which gave Boston a 7–6 win over Cincinnati. Fisk set records for durability behind the plate over a 24-season big-league career.

"G" is for the "Green Monster,"

Fenway's left-field wall.
The hits clanging off it
Ring a loud wake-up call.

BOSTON'S FENWAY PARK, opened in 1912, is the major leagues' oldest stadium, and its close, towering left-field fence, called the "Green Monster," is its outstanding feature. The wall stands an inviting 310 feet from home plate. It turns routine fly balls into hits and changes drives that would be home runs elsewhere into singles or doubles. Originally covered with advertising signs, it was first painted solid green in 1947. Seats were installed atop it for the 2003 season.

"H" is for Hooper,

A defensive gazelle.
On four pennant winners
He did his job well.

HARRY HOOPER joined the Red Sox in 1909 with a college degree, which was rare for a ballplayer of his era. He quickly became a regular as a leadoff hitter and right fielder. From 1910 through 1915 he teamed with center fielder Tris Speaker and left fielder Duffy Lewis to form what is still regarded as one of baseball's greatest outfields. Hooper was the only man to play on all four of the Red Sox's World Series champion teams (1912, 1915, 1916, and 1918) in the 20th century's second decade.

"I" is for "Idiots,"

The tongue-in-cheek name
The '04 champs used
To lighten up the game.

"J" is for Joe Wood,

Whose fastball had steam.
His 1912 season
Was a young pitcher's dream.

"SMOKEY" JOE WOOD, a right-handed pitcher, made the Red Sox as an 18-year-old in 1908 and quickly developed into a star. In 1912, at age 22, he had one of the best seasons of any pitcher ever, posting a 34–5 won-lost record, a 1.91 earned-run average, and 258 strikeouts. He then led the team in its World Series triumph over the New York Giants by winning three games, including the seventh-game clincher. Alas, the next year he injured his throwing-hand thumb during a fielding play, and while he pitched for several seasons more, he never recaptured his top form.

"K" is for Kinder,

He gave it a try,
But in his best seasons
The Sox came up shy.

ELLIS KINDER, a right-handed pitcher, didn't reach the major leagues until age 32, but once he got there he posted 102 victories over 12 seasons. His best year in Boston was 1949, when the Red Sox battled the Yankees down to the season's final day only to fall short by one game. He won 23 games that season and held the Yanks to a single run in seven innings in the head-to-head finale, which the team eventually lost, 5–3. He later excelled as a relief pitcher.

"L" is for Lynn,

Who arrived in a blaze,
Led the Sox to a pennant,
And won MVP praise.

FEW PLAYERS HAVE HAD A DEBUT CAMPAIGN AS GOOD AS FREDDIE LYNN'S. With the pennant-winning Red Sox in 1975, the California native hit .331, drove in 105 runs, and became the first player to capture both Rookie-of-the-Year and Most-Valuable-Player awards in the same season. Lynn, a center fielder, had other fine years—with the California Angels and the Baltimore Orioles as well as with the Red Sox—but none was as good as his first.

"M" is for Martinez,

Whose arm is a whip.
Few pitchers' deliveries
Have quite as much zip.

PEDRO MARTINEZ, from the Dominican Republic, has a slender build, but generates enough arm speed to make himself one of the dominant pitchers of the new century. In the first six seasons after coming to Boston in a 1997 trade with the Montreal Expos, he won 101 of his 129 decisions and captured the American League's Cy Young Award in 1999 and 2000. His competitive nature and strikeout flair have further endeared him to Boston fans.

"N" is for Nomar.

That's Garciaparra.
His towering home runs
Can hardly go "fartha."

ANTHONY NOMAR GARCIAPARRA is a rare good-fielding shortstop who also has power at the plate. In his first seven seasons after joining the Red Sox full time in 1997, he hit 25 or more home runs four times and won American League batting titles in 1999 (.357) and 2000 (.372). Garciaparra—who was traded to the Cubs in the summer of 2004—is married to Mia Hamm, an international women's soccer star.

"O" is for Ortiz,
Whose hits fueled the streak
That sent the Yanks reeling
And helped climb the peak.

DAVID ORTIZ, from the Dominican Republic, came to Boston as a free agent in 2003 and quickly established himself as a power-hitting force. He never shone brighter than in the team's comeback against the Yankees in the ALCS, winning Game 4 with a walk-off, twelfth-inning home run and driving in the winning run in the fourteenth inning of the marathon fifth game. His heroics earned the big first baseman and designated hitter the ALCS's Most Valuable Player award.

"P" is for Pesky,

Whose throw came too late.
Some people still ask,

"Did he hesitate?"

JOHNNY PESKY was the shortstop on the pennant-winning Red Sox team of 1946. He had an excellent major league career, but is famous mostly for the play on which the St. Louis Cardinals' Enos Slaughter scored from first base on a single to give his team the winning run in the seventh and deciding game of that year's World Series. Pesky took the relay from outfielder Leon Culberson and may have hesitated an instant before throwing the ball to home. Pesky said he didn't delay, but others said he did. Whatever the case may be, most observers agree that the throw wouldn't have arrived in time to catch the sliding Slaughter.

"Q" is for the question:
Why Lord, why oh why, Did Bill Buckner let That ground ball get by?

A BLUNDER EVEN MORE FAMOUS than Pesky's took place in the sixth game of the 1986 World Series, which pitted the Red Sox against the New York Mets. Boston led the Series three games to two and was ahead 5–3 going into the bottom of the tenth inning at Shea Stadium, but after the first two New York hitters were retired, the Mets scored a run on three singles and another on a wild pitch. Then, with a runner on second base, Mookie Wilson hit a bouncer through the legs of BILL BUCKNER, the Boston first baseman, and the winning run scored. The Mets went on to win the seventh game and the Series. Like Pesky, Buckner was an outstanding player, but is remembered mostly as a World Series "goat."

"R" is for Rice and Ramirez,

Who battered the fences
With line drives that shattered
Opponents' defenses.

JIM RICE and MANNY RAMIREZ were two of the best power hitters in recent Red Sox history. The muscular Rice played his entire 16-season career in Boston, hitting 382 home runs, driving in 100 or more runs eight times, and helping the team win the 1975 and 1986 pennants. Ramirez, an ex–Cleveland Indian, was signed as a free agent in the winter of 2000 and hit 41, 33, and 37 homers in his first three seasons with the Sox. He continued the pounding in 2004, leading the team with 43 regular-season homers and gaining Most Valuable Player honors in the World Series, during which he hit .412.

"S" is for Speaker.

So quick was his pace
That he played center field
Just behind second base.

TRISTAM SPEAKER was the best center fielder—and one of the best overall players—of the first half of the 20th century. He batted .345 in his 22 big-league seasons (1907–1928), the first 9 of which were with the Red Sox. His speed and timing allowed him to play his position unusually shallow even for the "dead ball" era; he dared batters to hit one over his head, and few could. His arm was so strong that his 448 career assists still stand as the most for any outfielder.

"T" is for Tiant,

Baseball's genial señor.
He showed hitters his back
And then closed the door.

LUIS TIANT, who was born in Cuba, dazzled major league hitters with his twisting deliveries for 19 seasons, 8 of which (1971–1978) were spent with the Red Sox. He had some of his best years in Boston, posting 122 of his 229 career victories there and winning 20 or more games in three different seasons (1973, 1974, and 1976). He was a popular player whose trademark was a postvictory cigar—Cuban, of course.

"U" is for Ugueth Urbina,

A rare double *U*.
And if that's not enough
There's a middle *U*, too.

UGUETH URBINA, from Venezuela, is a fastballing, right-handed relief pitcher who saved 40 games and won All-Star Game recognition with the 2002 Red Sox. The next season he left the team as a free agent and wound up starring in the bullpen for the World Series–winning Florida Marlins. His middle name is Urtain, making him the only player in major league history to have the initials U.U.U.

"V" is for Mo Vaughn,

Whose body was thick.
He handled a bat
Like a tiny toothpick.

MAURICE "MO" VAUGHN packed upwards of 275 pounds on his 6'1" frame, but was the leading Red Sox slugger during his tenure with the team (1991–1998). In his seven seasons as a Boston starter, Vaughn hit 226 home runs and drove in 100 or more runs four times. In 1995, when he hit .300 with 39 homers and 126 RBIs, he was voted the American League's most valuable player.

"W" is for Williams,

Whose picture-perfect swing
Made Fenway fans cheer
When his home runs took wing.

TED WILLIAMS was the greatest hitter in Red Sox history, and perhaps in all of baseball's as well. Combining superb physical coordination with an analytical approach to the batter's art, the "Splendid Splinter" had a career average of .344, 2,654 hits, and 521 home runs over 19 seasons ending in 1960—figures that would have been considerably higher had he not missed all or most of five seasons for military service in World War II and the Korean War. His .406 batting average in 1941 was the last time a major leaguer hit .400 or better for a full campaign. In his last turn at bat, at Fenway Park on September 26, 1960, he hit a home run.

"X" is for "Double X"

The great Jimmie Foxx.
Some of his best work
Was with the Red Sox.

JIMMIE FOXX succeeded Babe Ruth as baseball's premier power hitter, bashing 534 home runs in a career that spanned 21 years (1925–1945). Seven of those seasons (1936–1942) were with the Red Sox, including the 1938 campaign in which he hit 50 home runs and drove in 175. Foxx not only hit lots of homers, he also hit them hard and far. One of his blows shattered a seat in the distant reaches of Yankee Stadium.

"Y" is for Denton "Cy" Young,

Whose win total is why
The awards for best pitcher
Are nicknamed "the Cy."

"CY" (FOR "CYCLONE") YOUNG was baseball's all-time winningest pitcher; his career victory count of 511 isn't likely to be broken. A large, sturdy man, the right-hander played at a time (1890–1911) when starting pitchers commonly threw 40 or more complete games in a season, but he stood out even in that iron-man era. In his eight seasons with the Red Sox (1901–1908), he won 20 or more games six times, and his win total in Boston (192) was a team record that he later shared with Roger Clemens. Baseball's annual awards for the best pitcher in each league are named for him.

"Z" is for Yaz

That's Carl Yastrzemski.
For 23 seasons
His name topped the marquee.

CARL "YAZ" YASTRZEMSKI started out as a shortstop, but changed to the outfield upon joining the Red Sox and, over 23 seasons (1961–1983), became a fixture in front of Fenway Park's famous left-field wall. Yaz played in a record 3,308 games in a Boston uniform and tops the team's all-time list in seven batting categories. In 1967 he became the last player to win baseball's Triple Crown, leading the American League in hitting (.326), home runs (44), and runs batted in (121).

"A" is for **"At last!"**

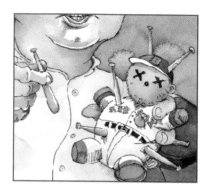

"B" is for **Babe Ruth**

"C" is for Roger **Clemens**

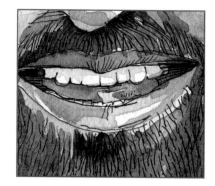

"D" is for Johnny **Damon**

"E" is for Dwight **Evans**

"F" is for Carlton "Pudge" **Fisk**

"G" is for "**Green Monster**"

"H" is for Harry **Hooper**

"J" is for **Joe Wood**

"K" is for Ellis **Kinder**

"L" is for Freddie **Lynn**

"M" is for Pedro **Martinez**

"N" is for **Nomar** Garciaparra

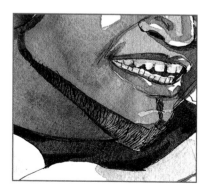

"O" is for David **Ortiz**

"P" is for Johnny **Pesky**

"Q" is for **Question (Bill Buckner)**

"R" is for Jim **Rice**

"R" is for Manny **Ramiraz**

"S" is for Tris **Speaker**

"T" is for Luis **Tiant**

"U" is for Ugueth **Urbina**

"V" is for Mo **Vaughn**

"W" is for Ted **Williams**

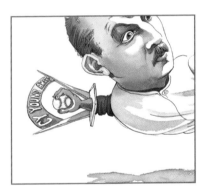

"X" is for Jimmy Foxx

"Y" is for Cy **Young**

"Z" is for Yastrzemski

"A" is for **Author**

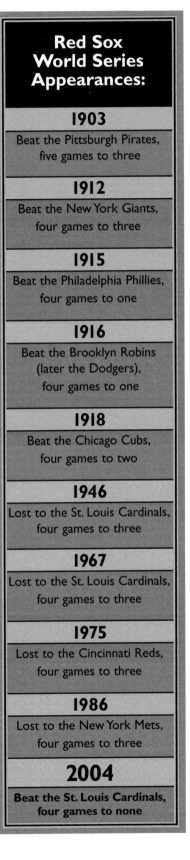

"I" is for **Illustrator**

Red Sox World Series Appearances:

1903
Beat the Pittsburgh Pirates, five games to three

1912
Beat the New York Giants, four games to three

1915
Beat the Philadelphia Phillies, four games to one

1916
Beat the Brooklyn Robins (later the Dodgers), four games to one

1918
Beat the Chicago Cubs, four games to two

1946
Lost to the St. Louis Cardinals, four games to three

1967
Lost to the St. Louis Cardinals, four games to three

1975
Lost to the Cincinnati Reds, four games to three

1986
Lost to the New York Mets, four games to three

2004
Beat the St. Louis Cardinals, four games to none

This book is available in quantity at special discounts for your group or organization. For further information, contact:

Triumph Books
601 South LaSalle St., Suite 500
Chicago, Illinois 60605
312. 939. 3330
Fax 312. 663. 3557

Printed in U.S.A.
ISBN-13: 978-1-57243-750-0
ISBN-10: 1-57243-750-2